Simple Maths books available in hardback
Boxes
Circles
Games (Number Games in paperback edition)
Number Puzzles
Printing
Railways

Simple Maths books available in paperback
Facts and figures
Numbers
Number Games
Number Puzzles

First paperback edition published 1999
First published in hardback in 1993 by
A & C Black (Publishers) Ltd
35 Bedford Row, London, WC1R 4JH
© 1993 A & C Black (Publishers) Ltd

A CIP record for this book is available from the British Library.
ISBN 0-7136-5271-3

Acknowledgements
Edited by Barbara Taylor
Mathematics consultant Mike Spooner

The photographer, author and publishers would
like to thank the following people whose help
and co-operation made this book possible:
the staff and pupils of Kenmont Primary School,
the Early Learning Centre, James Galt & Co Ltd.

Typeset by Rowland Phototypesetting Ltd,
Bury St Edmunds, Suffolk.
Printed and bound in Italy by L.E.G.O. Spa

Numbers

Rose Griffiths
Photographs by Peter Millard

A & C Black · London

How many numbers have you seen today?

I've got numbers on my clothes.

The number on my badge
tells you how old I am.

How old will
I be on my
next birthday?

Can you find your age here?

4

10

7

8

5

9

40

Shaun is making some numbers for crayon rubbing.

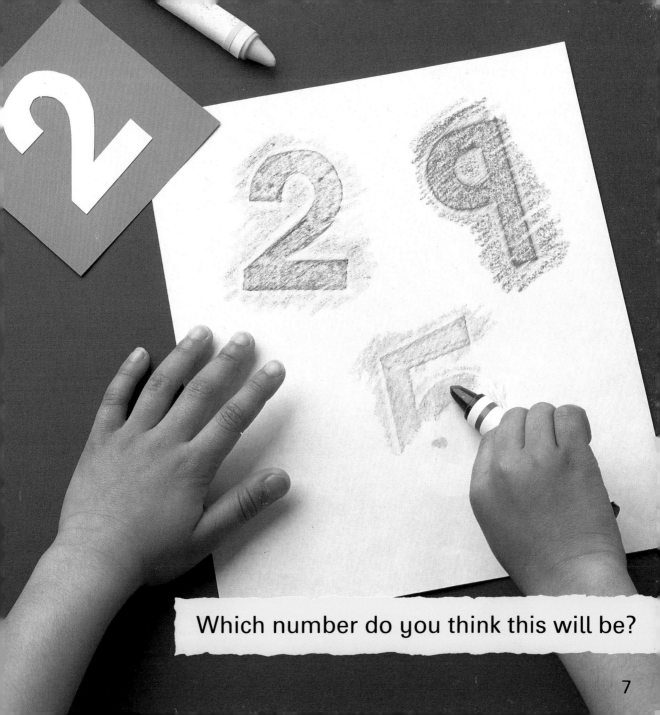

Which number do you think this will be?

Do you know which are letters and which are numbers?

a w r h i
l 0 d e g l
b f c 6 2 9
7 8 4
y 3 m 5 n
o

We use ten different numerals.

0 1 2 3 4 5 6 7 8 9

Why do you think there are ten?

We put numerals
together to make
bigger numbers.

10

Some languages use other numerals.

Gujarati numerals look like this.

૦ ૧ ૨ ૩ ૪ ૫ ૬ ૭ ૮ ૯

0 1 2 3 4 5 6 7 8 9

These are Roman numbers.

Can you find the number seven?

Amy has a digital alarm clock.

Where else have you seen numbers like these?

13

We can write one
numeral in many
different ways.

We use numbers when we count things.

We also use numbers
when we weigh things . . .

16

. . . and measure
how long they are.

Numbers help us tell
one thing from another.

My boat came first!

19

Some numbers help us find places.
I'm sending a letter to my friend.

Here's her front door.

54

Which numbers are important to you?

These are my size.

That's the day we're going on holiday.

More things to do

For these activities, you can use numbers from any language that you know.

1. Number spotting
Look out for numbers on things around you. You could keep a list or draw pictures of the things you see. You might want to look for just one number, such as your age, and see how many different places you can find it. Which is the biggest number you can find? Which numbers do you see most often? How are the numbers used?

2. Games with numbers
How many games do you know which use numbers? Practise a game you know, learn a new game, or make up a game of your own which uses numbers.

3. Number rubbing
Draw the shape of a number on card and cut it out. Put a piece of paper over the number and scribble evenly over the top with a wax crayon until the number shows through. You could use your number rubbings to decorate a maths folder, make a number frieze or make number patterns.

Find the page

This list shows you where to find some of the ideas in this book.

Pages 2, 3, 13, 16, 18, 19, 20, 21, 22, 23
Numbers around us

Pages 4, 5, 22, 23
Your own numbers

Pages 6, 7, 13, 14
Shapes of numbers

Page 8
Numbers or letters?

Pages 9, 10
Little and big numbers

Page 11
Gujarati numbers

Page 12
Roman numbers

Pages 15, 16, 17, 18, 19, 20, 21
Counting, measuring and finding things

Notes for parents and teachers

As you read this book with children, these notes will help you to explain the mathematical ideas behind the different activities.

Numbers around us   Pages 2, 3, 13, 16, 18–23

Numbers appear on many items around us, including buses, street signs, toys, games, calendars, clothes and food packaging. Numbers are symbols which represent real things and abstract concepts.

Personal numbers   Pages 4, 5, 22, 23

Important personal numbers to a child include their age, the date of their birthday, the number of people in their family, their shoe size or the phone number of a close friend. Children are more likely to be interested in numbers which mean something to them.

The shape of numbers   Pages 6, 7, 13, 14

A number can be written or printed in a variety of different ways. Encourage children to write numbers clearly. If they sometimes reverse their numerals, they may find it helpful to look at a ruler, a number line, a clock or the keys on a calculator for examples to copy.

Digital numbers consist of up to seven light bars. They are used on calculators, timers and videos.

Numbers, letters and numerals   Pages 8, 9, 10

We use letters to make words and numerals to make numbers. A word can be just one letter and a number just one numeral. The word 'digit' or 'figure' can be used instead of the word numeral. Letters and numerals, such as '5' and 's', may be mistaken for each other.

Different number systems   Pages 9, 10, 11, 12

Most people in the world use number systems based on grouping things in tens, probably because people have always used their fingers to count with. The numerals most of us use today developed from an early Hindu number system which included a zero. This meant that numbers of any size could be written using only the numerals 1, 2, 3, 4, 5, 6, 7, 8 and 9, plus the zero. The value of each numeral used in a number depends on its place in relation to the other numerals. This is called place value. For example, in 1304 the value of 3 is 300, while in 435, the value of 3 is 30.

The Roman number system (page 12) is built up in a completely different way, without using zero. The symbols it uses include I = 1, V = 5, X = 10, L = 50, C = 100, D = 500, and M = 1000.

Using numbers   Pages 15, 16, 17, 18, 19, 20, 21

Numbers are used for counting and when we measure things, such as time, money, temperature, length or capacity. They are also used (sometimes with letters) as a code or a label to distinguish one item from another. The numbers may have been issued in order, such as for a bank card or a car registration number, or chosen more arbitrarily. Some numbers, such as house numbers, page numbers or map references, help us locate things.

Cardinal and ordinal numbers   Pages 18, 19

The numbers we use for counting (1, 2, 3 . . .) are called cardinal numbers. Ordinal numbers (1st, 2nd, 3rd . . .) are the ones we use when we put things in order.